Greatest Ever

Baking

The All Time Top 20 Greatest Recipes

NOTE

This book uses metric and imperial measurements. Follow the same
units of measurement throughout; do not mix metric and imperial.
All spoon measurements are level: teaspoons are assumed to be 5 ml,
and tablespoons are assumed to be 15 ml. Unless otherwise stated,
milk is assumed to be full fat, eggs and individual vegetables such as
potatoes are medium, and pepper is freshly ground black pepper.

The times given for each recipe are an approximate guide only
because the preparation times may differ according to the techniques
used by different people and the cooking times may vary as a result
of the type of oven used. The preparation times include marinating,
chilling and freezing times, where appropriate.

Recipes using raw or very lightly cooked eggs should be
avoided by infants, the elderly, pregnant women, convalescents,
and anyone suffering from an illness.

CONTENTS

INTRODUCTION

Baking is an incredibly satisfying activity. You start with a few shapeless ingredients – flour, sugar, fat and eggs – and turn them into beautiful mouthwatering cakes, biscuits, pies, breads and desserts to delight your family and friends.

In just 20 recipes, you are introduced to all the skills of baking and discover how to create some of the best-loved cakes, biscuits, scones and flans. Clear, step-by-step instructions guide you through the techniques needed to mastermind all those baking favourites that have been savoured and enjoyed from generation to generation.

CAKE-BAKING AND STORAGE

Do not be too impatient and open the oven door while your cake is baking. Wait until it has nearly finished cooking before testing to see if it is ready. When cooked, the cake will have shrunk away from the sides of the tin slightly. Press the centre of the top lightly with your fingertips – it should spring back at once. Alternatively, push a fine metal skewer into the centre of the cake – if it comes out clean, the cake is done.

Leave the cake in its tin to cool slightly before turning out on to a wire rack to cool completely. Store the finished cake in an airtight container.

Above: The dried ingredients used in cake-baking should be measured out very carefully. Use good quality, fresh ingredients to achieve the best results.

FAMILY FAVOURITES

So what's to stop you baking your way into your family's good books and impressing your friends? Even mundane coffee breaks and children's packed lunches will be much more popular with the offer of a piece of home-baked Golden Fruit Cake or some delicious Treacle Scones to go with them.

The tasty Spiced Apple Gingerbread and Classic Carrot Cake are more down-to-earth, cut-and-come-again treats to keep in the cake tin – if you can – to satisfy an attack of the munchies.

The Sultana & Cherry Scones and Spicy Fruit Loaf are comfortingly familiar and excellent served with morning coffee or afternoon tea. If you are new to baking you'll be pleasantly surprised by how straightforward they are to make.

Even in a small selection of recipes like this, there have to be some chocolate treats for the chocoholics in your life. Few will be able to resist a piece of luscious Chocolate & Pear Sponge or Sandwich Cake with Chocolate Topping.

To round off a meal on a high note, the Mixed Fruit Pavlova and Raspberry & Cream Shortbread are simple puddings with a guaranteed 'Wow!' factor.

GOLDEN RULES OF BAKING

scales

box grater

measuring spoons

Making cakes

Clear, step-by-step instructions guide you through the measuring, mixing and baking of each recipe. Baking calls for precision and there are some ground rules you should always follow:

★ Make sure you read the recipe from start to finish so you know what ingredients and cake tins you need.

★ Weigh out all the ingredients accurately and do any preparation, such as grating, chopping or tin greasing and lining, before you start mixing.

★ Keep cake ingredients at room temperature.

★ Mix thoroughly, with the firmness or delicacy recommended, and for as long as the recipe requires.

★ Use a metal spoon or plastic spatula for folding flour into cake mixtures, sugar into whisked egg whites or egg whites into the rest of the ingredients.

★ Always use the size and shape of tin recommended in the recipe, otherwise the cake may not cook properly in the time allowed.

Making pastry for tarts

When making pastry for the flans and tarts in this book, follow this basic method:

1 Sift the dry ingredients into a large mixing bowl, add the diced fat and toss it through the flour.

2 Gently rub the fat between your fingertips, until the mixture resembles fine breadcrumbs. To make light pastry, raise your hands as you rub the fat into the flour to aerate the mixture as it falls back into the bowl.

Left: A set of measuring spoons ensures accurate and consistent measurements.

8

pecan nuts

3 Lightly bind the mixture with iced water or other specified liquid, using just enough to form the crumbs into a ball of soft but not sticky dough. Wrap the dough in clingfilm and chill for at least 30 minutes before rolling out.

dark chocolate

Using chocolate

Bittersweet, dark chocolate is most popular for baking. Dark chocolate with between 50 and 72 per cent cocoa solids is suitable for everyday cooking.

Break the chocolate into small, equal-sized pieces and put them in a heatproof bowl. Sit the bowl over a pan of simmering water, with its base clear of the water. As the chocolate starts to melt, stir gently until smooth. Make sure that no water splashes into the molten chocolate or it will solidify.

To melt the chocolate in a microwave, place small pieces in a microwave-proof bowl. Timing varies according to the type and quantity of chocolate. As a guide, 125 g/ 4½ oz dark chocolate takes 2 minutes on High to melt; white or milk chocolate takes 2–3 minutes on Medium.

When the time is up, stir the chocolate and leave to stand for a few minutes before stirring again. If necessary return the bowl to the microwave for a further 30 seconds.

eggs

Setting chocolate

Chocolate sets best at 18°C/65°F, although it will set more slowly in a slightly warmer room. If set in the refrigerator it may develop a white bloom and be very brittle. If possible, set chocolate decorations in a cool room.

oranges

Right: Melted chocolate solidifies into a mouth-watering cake topping.

9

Before you start baking any of the cakes, scones, flans or breads in this book you will need to check that you have some basic equipment.

spatula

wooden spoon

E Q U I P M E N T

mixing bowl

basin

ramekin dishes

Scales

As the precise measurement of ingredients is important in baking, it is hard to manage without scales. Make sure that the dial or display is clear enough to read easily.

Measuring jug

This is handy for measuring an exact quantity of liquid. A 1.2-litre/2-pint size is the most useful.

Measuring spoons

A full set of measuring spoons usually includes a ¼ teaspoon, ½ teaspoon, 1 teaspoon and 1 tablespoon. They are useful for measuring small amounts of raising agents and spices.

Sieve

It is a good idea to keep a separate sieve for sifting dry ingredients, such as flour and icing sugar, to remove the lumps and add air.

Mixing bowl

A large, rounded stainless steel, glass, plastic or glazed ceramic bowl is invaluable for mixing ingredients.

Basins

You will need several smaller basins for beating eggs or whipping cream, and for assembling ingredients before mixing.

Wooden spoons

A large, flat, wooden spoon is good for creaming butter and sugar together.

measuring jug

Plastic spatulas

These are used for folding in ingredients and for scraping out the last remnants of the mixture from the bowl.

Cake tins

Always buy the best quality tins you can afford: non-stick surfaces are helpful but still require a light coating of oil. Make sure you wash and dry the tins well before storing. Check the recipe first to find out what shape and size of cake or loaf tin you need.

Flan tins

A metal flan tin cooks the pastry more crisply than glass or ceramic dishes. Loose-based tins with removable sides are the best. A 20-cm/8-inch flan tin is the most useful size.

Baking sheets and trays

A good heavyweight baking sheet and tray are essential because they will not buckle in the oven.

Cooling rack

A cooling rack allows the steam to escape from a baked item and prevents it from becoming soggy.

Rolling pin

To roll pastry well you need a heavy, smooth rolling pin. In emergencies a milk bottle will do but it does not give an even rolling.

Palette knife

This long-bladed, flexible knife is used for spreading whipped cream and icing.

Pastry brush

A brush is useful for dusting excess flour from pastry, applying an egg or milk glaze or greasing tins. Make sure you wash and dry the brush well, or the bristles will start to fall out.

Pastry cutters

These are available in a range of shapes and sizes, fluted and plain, and are used for stamping out scones and biscuits. Make sure you wash and dry them well after use to prevent them rusting.

baking trays

food mixer

pastry brushes

pastry cutters

11

SANDWICH CAKE WITH CHOCOLATE TOPPING

>Serves 8–10   >Preparation time: 1 hour   >Cooking time: 20 minutes

INGREDIENTS

125 g/4½ oz soft margarine

125 g/4½ oz caster sugar

2 eggs

1 tbsp golden syrup

125 g/4½ oz self-raising flour, sieved

2 tbsp cocoa powder, sieved

FILLING AND TOPPING

50 g/1¾ oz icing sugar, sieved

2 tbsp butter

100 g/3½ oz white or milk cooking chocolate

a little milk or white chocolate, melted (optional)

METHOD

1 Lightly grease two 18-cm/7-inch shallow cake tins.

2 Place all of the cake ingredients in a large mixing bowl and beat with a wooden spoon or electric hand whisk to form a smooth mixture.

3 Divide the mixture between the prepared tins and level the tops. Bake the cake layers in a preheated oven, 190°C/375°F/Gas Mark 5, for 20 minutes, or until springy to the touch. Cool for a few minutes in the tins before transferring to a wire rack to cool completely.

4 To make the filling, beat the icing sugar and butter together in a bowl until light and fluffy. Melt the cooking chocolate and beat half into the icing mixture. Use the filling to sandwich the 2 cakes together.

5 Spread the remaining melted cooking chocolate over the top of the cake. Pipe circles of melted milk or white chocolate, if using, and feather into the cooking chocolate with a cocktail stick. Leave to set before serving.

SPICED BREAD & BUTTER PUDDING

>Serves 6   >Preparation time: 1 hour   >Cooking time: 40–45 minutes

INGREDIENTS
200 g/7 oz white bread, sliced

4 tbsp butter, softened

25 g/1 oz sultanas

25 g/1 oz mixed peel

½ tsp ground mixed spice

CUSTARD
600 ml/1 pint milk

4 egg yolks

75 g/2¼ oz caster sugar

METHOD
1 Grease a 1.2-litre/2-pint ovenproof dish.

2 Remove the crusts from the bread, if liked, spread with butter and cut into quarters.

3 Arrange half of the buttered bread slices in the prepared ovenproof dish. Sprinkle half of the sultanas and mixed peel over the top of the bread.

4 Place the remaining bread slices over the fruit, then sprinkle over the reserved fruit.

5 To make the custard, bring the milk almost to the boil in a saucepan. Whisk together the egg yolks and the sugar in a bowl, then pour in the warm milk.

6 Strain the warm custard through a sieve. Pour the custard over the bread slices.

7 Leave to stand for 30 minutes, then sprinkle with the ground mixed spice.

8 Place the ovenproof dish in a roasting tin half-filled with hot water.

9 Bake in a preheated oven, 200°C/400°F/Gas Mark 6, for 40–45 minutes, or until the pudding has just set. Serve warm.

CLASSIC CARROT CAKE

>Makes 12 bars >Preparation time: 10 minutes >Cooking time: 20–25 minutes

INGREDIENTS

125 g/4½ oz self-raising flour

pinch of salt

1 tsp ground cinnamon

125 g/4½ oz soft brown sugar

2 eggs

100 ml/3½ fl oz sunflower oil

125 g/4½ oz carrot, peeled and finely grated

25 g/1 oz desiccated coconut

25 g/1 oz walnuts, chopped

walnut pieces, for decoration

ICING

4 tbsp butter, softened

50 g/1¼ oz full-fat soft cheese

225 g/8 oz icing sugar, sieved

1 tsp lemon juice

METHOD

1 Lightly grease a 20-cm/8-inch square cake tin and line with baking paper.

2 Sieve the flour, salt and ground cinnamon into a large bowl and stir in the brown sugar. Add the eggs and oil to the dry ingredients and mix well.

3 Stir in the grated carrot, desiccated coconut and chopped walnuts.

4 Pour the mixture into the prepared tin and bake in a preheated oven, 180°C/350°F/Gas Mark 4, for 20–25 minutes, or until just firm to the touch. Leave to cool in the tin.

5 Meanwhile, make the icing. In a bowl, beat together the butter, full-fat soft cheese, icing sugar and lemon juice until the mixture is fluffy and creamy.

6 Turn the cake out of the tin, spread with the icing, and cut into 12 bars or slices. Decorate with walnut pieces.

LEMON SPONGE CAKE

> Serves 8 > Preparation time: 1 hour > Cooking time: 45 minutes–1 hour

INGREDIENTS

200 g/7 oz plain flour

2 tsp baking powder

200 g/7 oz caster sugar

4 eggs

150 ml/5 fl oz soured cream

grated rind 1 large lemon

4 tbsp lemon juice

150 ml/5 fl oz sunflower oil

SYRUP

4 tbsp icing sugar

3 tbsp lemon juice

METHOD

1 Lightly grease a 20-cm/8-inch loose-bottomed round cake tin and line the base with baking paper.

2 Sieve the flour and baking powder into a mixing bowl and stir in the caster sugar.

3 In a separate mixing bowl, whisk the eggs, soured cream, lemon rind, lemon juice and sunflower oil together.

4 Pour the egg mixture into the dry ingredients and mix well until evenly combined.

5 Pour the mixture into the prepared tin and bake in a preheated oven, 180°C/350°F/Gas Mark 4, for 45–60 minutes until risen and golden brown.

6 Meanwhile, to make the syrup, mix together the icing sugar and lemon juice in a small saucepan. Stir over a low heat until just beginning to bubble and turn syrupy.

7 As soon as the cake comes out of the oven, prick the surface with a fine skewer, then brush the syrup over the top. Leave the cake to cool completely in the tin before turning out and serving.

GOLDEN FRUIT CAKE

>Serves 8–10 >Preparation time: 1 hour >Cooking time: 1 hour

INGREDIENTS

100 g/3½ oz butter, softened

100g/3½ oz caster sugar

2 eggs, beaten

50 g/1¾ oz self-raising flour, sieved

100 g/3½ oz polenta

1 tsp baking powder

225 g/8 oz mixed dried fruit

25 g/1 oz pine kernels

grated rind of 1 lemon

4 tbsp lemon juice

2 tbsp milk

METHOD

1 Grease an 18-cm/7-inch cake tin and line the base with baking paper.

2 In a bowl, whisk together the butter and sugar until light and fluffy.

3 Whisk in the beaten eggs a little at a time, whisking well after each addition.

4 Fold the flour, polenta and baking powder into the mixture until well blended.

5 Stir in the mixed dried fruit, pine kernels, grated lemon rind, lemon juice and milk.

6 Spoon the mixture into the prepared tin and level the surface.

7 Bake in a preheated oven, 180°C/350°F/Gas Mark 4, for 1 hour, or until a skewer inserted into the centre of the cake comes out clean.

8 Leave the cake to cool in the tin before turning out.

SPICY FRUIT LOAF

>Makes a 900 g/2 lb loaf   >Preparation time: 1 hour   >Cooking time: 1–1¼ hours

INGREDIENTS

350 g/12 oz plain flour

pinch of salt

1 tbsp baking powder

1 tbsp ground cinnamon

150 g/5½ oz butter, cut into small pieces

125 g/4½ oz soft brown sugar

175 g/6 oz currants

finely grated rind of 1 orange

5–6 tbsp orange juice

6 tbsp milk

2 eggs, lightly beaten

METHOD

1 Grease a 900-g/2-lb loaf tin and line the base smoothly with baking paper.

2 Sieve the flour, salt, baking powder and ground cinnamon into a bowl. Then rub in the pieces of butter with your fingers, until the mixture resembles coarse breadcrumbs.

3 Stir in the sugar, currants and orange rind. Beat the orange juice, milk and eggs together and add to the dry ingredients. Mix well together.

4 Spoon the mixture into the prepared tin. Make a slight dip in the middle of the mixture to help it rise evenly.

5 Bake in a preheated oven, 180°C/350°F/Gas Mark 4, for about 1–1¼ hours, or until a fine metal skewer inserted into the centre of the loaf comes out clean.

6 Leave the loaf to cool before turning out of the tin. Transfer to a wire rack and leave to cool completely before slicing.

CRANBERRY & ALMOND TART

›Serves 8–10 ›Preparation time: 1½ hours ›Cooking time: 1½ hours

INGREDIENTS

PASTRY

150 g/5½ oz plain flour

125 g/4½ oz caster sugar

125 g/4½ oz butter, cut into small pieces

1 tbsp water

FILLING

200 g/7 oz unsalted butter

200g/7 oz caster sugar

1 egg

2 egg yolks

40 g/1½ oz plain flour, sieved

175 g/6 oz ground almonds

4 tbsp double cream

410 g/14½ oz canned apricot halves, drained

125 g/4½ oz fresh cranberries

METHOD

1 To make the pastry, place the flour and sugar in a bowl and rub in the butter with your fingers. Add the water and work the mixture together until a soft dough has formed. Wrap and chill for 30 minutes.

2 On a lightly floured surface, roll out the dough and line a 24-cm/9½-inch loose-bottomed flan tin. Prick the pastry with a fork and chill for 30 minutes.

3 Line the pastry case with foil and baking beans and bake in a preheated oven, 190°C/375°F/Gas Mark 5, for 15 minutes. Remove the foil and baking beans and cook for a further 10 minutes.

4 To make the filling, cream together the butter and sugar until light and fluffy. Beat in the egg and egg yolks, then stir in the flour, almonds and cream.

5 Place the apricot halves and cranberries on the bottom of the pastry case and spoon the filling over the top.

6 Bake in the oven for about 1 hour, or until the topping is just set. Leave to cool slightly, then serve warm or cold.

SULTANA & CHERRY SCONES

>Makes 8 >Preparation time: 30 minutes >Cooking time: 8–10 minutes

INGREDIENTS

225 g/8 oz self-raising flour

1 tbsp caster sugar

pinch of salt

75 g/2¾ oz butter, cut into small pieces

40 g/1½ oz glacé cherries, chopped

40 g/1½ oz sultanas

1 egg, beaten

4 tbsp milk

METHOD

1 Lightly grease a baking tray.

2 Sieve the flour, sugar and salt into a mixing bowl and rub in the butter with your fingers until the mixture resembles breadcrumbs.

3 Stir in the glacé cherries and sultanas. Add the egg.

4 Reserve 1 tablespoon of the milk for glazing, then add the remainder to the mixture. Mix together to form a soft dough.

5 On a lightly floured surface, roll out the dough to a thickness of 2 cm/¾ inch and cut out 8 scones, using a 5-cm/2-inch cutter.

6 Place the scones on to the baking tray and brush with the reserved milk.

7 Bake in a preheated oven, 220°C/425°F/Gas Mark 7, for 8–10 minutes, or until the scones are golden brown.

8 Leave to cool on a wire rack, then serve split in half spread with butter.

MINI MERINGUES

>Makes about 13 >Preparation time: 20 minutes >Cooking time: 1½ hours

INGREDIENTS

4 egg whites

pinch of salt

125 g/4½ oz granulated sugar

125 g/4½ oz caster sugar

300 ml/10 fl oz double cream, lightly whipped

METHOD

1 Line 3 baking trays with baking paper.

2 In a large, clean bowl, whisk together the egg whites and salt until they are stiff, using an electric hand-held whisk or a balloon whisk. (You should be able to turn the bowl upside down without any movement from the whisked egg whites.)

3 Whisk in the granulated sugar a little at a time; at this stage, the meringue should start to look glossy.

4 Sprinkle in the caster sugar a little at a time and continue whisking until all the sugar has been incorporated and the meringue is thick, white and stands in tall peaks.

5 Transfer the meringue mixture to a piping bag fitted with a 2-cm/¾-inch star nozzle. Pipe about 26 small whirls on to the prepared baking trays.

6 Bake in a preheated oven, 120°C/250°F/Gas Mark ½, for 1½ hours, or until the meringues are pale golden in colour and can be easily lifted off the paper. Leave them to cool in the turned-off oven overnight.

7 Just before serving, sandwich the meringues together in pairs with the cream and arrange on a serving plate.

MIXED FRUIT PAVLOVA

> Serves 6 > Preparation time: 1¼ hours > Cooking time: 1¼ hours

INGREDIENTS

3 egg whites

pinch of salt

175 g/6 oz caster sugar

300 ml/10 fl oz double cream, lightly whipped

fresh fruit of your choice, such as raspberries, strawberries, peaches, passion fruit and cape gooseberries

METHOD

1 Line a baking sheet with baking paper.

2 Whisk the egg whites with the salt in a large bowl until they form soft peaks.

3 Whisk in the sugar a little at a time, whisking well after each addition until all of the sugar has been incorporated.

4 Spoon three-quarters of the meringue on to the baking sheet, forming a round 20 cm/ 8 inches in diameter.

5 Place spoonfuls of the remaining meringue all around the edge of the round so they join up to make a nest shape.

6 Bake in a preheated oven, 140°C/275°F/Gas Mark 1, for 1¼ hours.

7 Turn the heat off, but leave the pavlova in the oven until completely cold.

8 Place the pavlova on a serving dish. Spread with the lightly whipped cream, then arrange the fresh fruit on top.

SPICED APPLE GINGERBREAD

>Makes 12 bars >Preparation time: 1¼ hours >Cooking time: 30–35 minutes

INGREDIENTS

150 g/5½ oz butter

175 g/6 oz soft brown sugar

2 tbsp black treacle

225 g/8 oz plain flour

1 tsp baking powder

2 tsp bicarbonate of soda

2 tsp ground ginger

150 ml/5 fl oz milk

1 egg, beaten

2 dessert apples, peeled, chopped and coated with 1 tbsp lemon juice

METHOD

1 Grease a 23-cm/9-inch square cake tin and line with baking paper.

2 Melt the butter, sugar and treacle in a saucepan over a low heat and leave the mixture to cool.

3 Sieve the flour, baking powder, bicarbonate of soda and ginger into a mixing bowl.

4 Stir in the milk, beaten egg and cooled buttery liquid, followed by the chopped apples coated with the lemon juice.

5 Mix everything together gently, then pour the mixture into the prepared tin.

6 Bake in a preheated oven, 160°C/325°F/Gas Mark 3, for 30–35 minutes, or until the cake has risen and a fine skewer inserted into the centre comes out clean.

7 Leave the cake to cool in the tin before turning out and cutting into 12 bars.

MIXED FRUIT CRUMBLE

>Serves 4   >Preparation time: 10 minutes   >Cooking time: 50 minutes

INGREDIENTS

2 mangoes, sliced

1 pawpaw, seeded and sliced

225 g/8 oz fresh pineapple, cubed

1½ tsp ground ginger

100 g/3½ oz margarine

100 g/3½ oz light brown sugar

175 g/6 oz plain flour

50 g/1¼ oz desiccated coconut, plus extra
to decorate

METHOD

1 Place the fruit in a pan with ½ tsp of the ginger, 30 g/1 oz of the margarine and 50 g/1¾ oz of the sugar. Cook over a low heat for 10 minutes, until the fruit softens. Spoon the fruit into the base of a shallow ovenproof dish.

2 Mix the flour and remaining ginger together. Rub in the remaining margarine until the mixture resembles fine breadcrumbs. Stir in the remaining sugar and the coconut and spoon over the fruit to cover completely.

3 Cook the crumble in a preheated oven, 180°C/350°F/Gas Mark 4, for about 40 minutes, or until the top is crisp. Decorate with a sprinkling of desiccated coconut and serve.

LEMON CREAM BUTTERFLIES

>Makes 12 >Preparation time: 30 minutes >Cooking time: 15 minutes

INGREDIENTS

125 g/4½ oz soft margarine

125 g/4½ oz caster sugar

150 g/5½ oz self-raising flour

2 large eggs

2 tbsp cocoa powder

25 g/1 oz dark chocolate, melted

icing sugar, to dust

LEMON BUTTER CREAM

100 g/3½ oz unsalted butter, softened

225 g/8 oz icing sugar, sieved

grated rind of ½ lemon

1 tbsp lemon juice

METHOD

1 Place 12 paper cases in a muffin pan. Place all of the ingredients for the cakes, except for the melted chocolate, in a large mixing bowl and beat with electric beaters until the mixture is just smooth. Beat in the chocolate.

2 Spoon equal amounts of the cake mixture into each paper case, filling them three-quarters full. Bake in a preheated oven, 180°C/350°F/Gas Mark 4, for 15 minutes, or until springy to the touch. Transfer the cakes to a wire rack and leave to cool.

3 To make the lemon butter cream, place the butter in a mixing bowl and beat until fluffy, then gradually beat in the icing sugar. Beat in the lemon rind and gradually add the lemon juice, beating well.

4 When cold, cut the top off each cake, using a serrated knife. Cut each top in half.

5 Spread or pipe the butter cream icing over the cut surface of each cake and push the 2 cut pieces of cake top into the icing to form wings. Sprinkle with icing sugar.

CHOCOLATE & PEAR SPONGE

>Serves 6   >Preparation time: 1¼ hours   >Cooking time: 1 hour

INGREDIENTS

175 g/6 oz butter, softened

175 g/6 oz soft brown sugar

3 eggs, beaten

150 g/5½ oz self-raising flour

2 tbsp cocoa powder

2 tbsp milk

2 small pears, peel, cored and sliced

METHOD

1 Grease a 23-cm/8-inch loose-bottomed cake tin and line the base with baking parchment.

2 In a bowl, cream together the butter and soft brown sugar until pale and fluffy.

3 Gradually add the beaten eggs to the mixture, beating well after each addition.

4 Sieve the self-raising flour and cocoa powder into the creamed mixture and fold in gently until all of the ingredients are combined.

5 Stir in the milk, then spoon the mixture into the prepared tin. Level the surface with the back of a spoon or a knife.

6 Arrange the pear slices on top of the sponge mixture in a radiating pattern.

7 Bake in a preheated oven, 180°C/350°F/Gas Mark 4, for about 1 hour, or until the sponge is just firm to the touch.

8 Leave the sponge to cool in the tin, then transfer to a wire rack to cool completely before serving.

BUTTERY LEMON FLAN

>Serves 8 >Preparation time: 1½ hours >Cooking time: 50 minutes

INGREDIENTS

PASTRY

150 g/5½ oz plain flour

25 g/1 oz caster sugar

125 g/4½ oz butter, cut into small pieces

1 tbsp water

icing sugar, for dusting

FILLING

150 ml/5 fl oz double cream

100 g/3½ oz caster sugar

4 eggs

grated rind of 3 lemons

12 tbsp lemon juice

METHOD

1 To make the pastry, place the flour and sugar in a bowl and rub in the butter using your fingers. Add the water and mix until a soft dough has formed. Wrap the dough and chill for 30 minutes.

2 On a lightly floured surface, roll out the dough and line a 24-cm/9½-inch loose-bottomed flan tin. Prick the pastry with a fork and chill for 30 minutes.

3 Line the pastry case with foil and baking beans and bake in a preheated oven, 190°C/375°F/Gas Mark 5, for 15 minutes. Remove the foil and baking beans and cook for a further 15 minutes.

4 To make the filling, whisk the cream, sugar, eggs, lemon rind and juice together. Place the pastry case, still in its tin, on a baking tray and pour in the filling.

5 Bake in the oven for about 20 minutes, or until just set. Leave to cool, then lightly dust with icing sugar before serving.

TREACLE SCONES

>Serves 8   >Preparation time: 15 minutes   >Cooking time: 8–10 minutes

INGREDIENTS

225 g/8 oz self-raising flour

1 tbsp caster sugar

pinch of salt

6 tbsp butter, chilled and cut into small pieces

1 dessert apple, peeled, cored and chopped

1 egg, beaten

2 tbsp black treacle

5 tbsp milk

METHOD

1 Lightly grease a baking tray with butter.

2 Sieve the flour, sugar and salt into a bowl.

3 Add the butter and rub it in with your fingertips until the mixture resembles fine breadcrumbs.

4 Stir the chopped apple into the mixture until thoroughly combined.

5 Mix the beaten egg, treacle and milk together in a jug. Add the mixture to the dry ingredients and mix well to form a soft dough.

6 On a lightly floured work surface, roll out the dough to a thickness of 2 cm/¼ inch. Cut out 8 scones, using a 5-cm/2-inch cutter.

7 Arrange the treacle scones on the prepared baking tray and bake in a preheated oven, 220°C/425°F/Gas Mark 7, for 8–10 minutes.

8 Transfer the scones to a wire rack and leave to cool slightly. Serve split in half and spread with butter.

BAKED APPLE & SULTANA PUDDING

>Serves 6 >Preparation time: 15 minutes >Cooking time: 40–45 minutes

INGREDIENTS

450 g/1 lb cooking apples, peeled, cored and sliced

75 g/2¾ oz granulated sugar

1 tbsp lemon juice

50 g/1¾ oz sultanas

75 g/2¾ oz butter

75 g/2¾ oz caster sugar

1 egg, beaten

150 g/5½ oz self-raising flour

3 tbsp milk

25 g/1 oz flaked almonds

custard or double cream, to serve

METHOD

1 Grease an 850-ml/1½-pint ovenproof dish.

2 Mix the apples with the sugar, lemon juice and sultanas. Spoon the mixture into the greased dish.

3 In a mixing bowl, cream the butter and caster sugar together until pale. Add the egg, a little at a time.

4 Carefully fold in the self-raising flour and stir in the milk, which should give the mixture a soft, dropping consistency.

5 Spread the mixture over the apples and sprinkle with the flaked almonds.

6 Bake in a preheated oven, 180°C/350°F/Gas Mark 4, for 40–45 minutes, or until the sponge is golden brown.

7 Serve the pudding piping hot, accompanied by custard or double cream

RASPBERRY & CREAM SHORTBREAD

>Serves 8 >Preparation time: 40 minutes >Cooking time: 15 minutes

INGREDIENTS

175 g/6 oz self-raising flour

100 g/3½ oz butter, cut into cubes

75 g/2¾ oz caster sugar

1 egg yolk

1 tbsp rose water

600 ml/1 pint whipping cream, lightly whipped

225 g/8 oz raspberries, plus a few
for decoration

TO DECORATE

icing sugar

METHOD

1 Lightly grease 2 baking sheets.

2 To make the shortbreads, sieve the flour into a mixing bowl. Rub the butter into the flour with your fingers until the mixture resembles breadcrumbs.

3 Stir the sugar, egg yolk and rose water into the mixture and bring together with your fingers to form a soft dough. Divide the dough in half.

4 Roll each piece of dough to a 20-cm/8-inch round and lift each one on to a prepared baking sheet. Crimp the edges of the dough.

5 Bake in a preheated oven, 190°C/375°F/Gas Mark 5, for 15 minutes, or until lightly golden. Transfer the shortcakes to a wire rack and leave to cool.

6 Mix the cream with the raspberries and spoon on top of one of the shortbreads. Top with the other shortbread round, dust with a little icing sugar and decorate with the extra raspberries you kept back.

BERRY CHEESECAKE

❯Serves 8 ❯Preparation time: 2½ hours ❯Cooking time: 5 minutes

INGREDIENTS

BASE

75 g/2¾ oz margarine

175 g/6 oz oatmeal biscuits

50 g/1¾ oz desiccated coconut

FILLING

9 tbsp cold water

1½ tsp vegetarian gelatine

125 ml/4 fl oz evaporated milk

1 egg

75 g/2¾ oz soft light brown sugar

450 g/1 lb soft cream cheese

350 g/12 oz mixed berries

2 tbsp clear honey, for drizzling

METHOD

1 Place the margarine in a saucepan and heat until melted. Put the biscuits in a food processor and process until thoroughly crushed. Alternatively, crush finely with a rolling pin. Stir the biscuit crumbs into the margarine, together with the coconut.

2 Lightly grease a 20-cm/8-inch springform tin and line the base with baking parchment. Press the biscuit mixture evenly into the tin. Set aside in the refrigerator to chill while you prepare the filling for the cheesecake.

3 To make the filling, put the water in a pan and sprinkle the gelatine into it. Stir to dissolve. Bring to the boil and boil for 2 minutes. Leave to cool slightly.

4 Put the milk, egg, sugar and soft cream cheese in a bowl and beat until smooth. Stir in 50 g/1¾ oz of the berries. Add the gelatine in a stream, stirring constantly.

5 Spread the mixture on the biscuit base and return to the refrigerator to chill for 2 hours, or until set.

6 Remove the berry cheesecake from the tin and transfer it to a large serving plate. Arrange the remaining berries on top of the cheesecake, drizzle the honey over the top and serve.